JOLTIN' JOE BASEBALL HERO

Luke Jensen

Cover and all interior photos © CORBIS/Bettman,
except page 35: © CORBIS/AFP.

Designed by Judy Holloway.

Cover design by Michelle Donus.

Produced by Infinity Plus One.

Printed in the United States of America.

ISBN- 0-8167-6579-0

10 9 8 7 6 5 4 3 2 1

*

It was a cool afternoon on May 15, 1941. The New York Yankees were struggling with 14 wins and 14 losses. The team wasn't hitting well, and neither was their star, Joe DiMaggio. Joe came up to bat in the bottom of the first inning trying to break out of a slump. He had gotten just 9 hits in his last 39 at bats and had been held hitless in the previous two games.

DiMaggio stepped into the batter's box and squared off against the Chicago White Sox left-hander Edgar Smith. There were two outs, and Phil Rizzuto was on second. Joe lined a single to left field, and Rizzuto scored.

For the next 55 games, Joe DiMaggio would hit safely in every single game he played, setting an incredible baseball record many experts believe will never be broken.

*

Joseph Paul DiMaggio was born on November 25, 1914, in Martinez, California. His father, Giuseppe ("Joseph" in Italian), had arrived in the United States from Italy in 1902. His mother, Rosalie, arrived a year later, bringing their young daughter, Nellie, with her.

The DiMaggios traveled halfway across the world on the recommendation of relatives and friends who had described the California climate as being similar to Italy's. Giuseppe had been a fisherman in Sicily and continued this trade in America. Like many European immigrants, he hoped that America would be the land of opportunity for him and his family.

The DiMaggio family settled in the North Beach section of San Francisco on a high hill overlooking Fisherman's Wharf. Even in the early 1900's, Fisherman's Wharf was famous for its tourist trade, restaurants, and shops. It was also an important center of the fishing trade, and most of the 250 members of the crab-fishing fleet lived on the hill looking down on the wharf.

There was always someone to play with in the DiMaggio family because Joe had lots of brothers and sisters. Nellie was the oldest, and Mamie followed in 1903. Thomas was born in 1905, Marie in 1906, Michael in 1908, Frances in 1910, Vincent in 1912, and then Joe in 1914. Joe had one younger brother, Dominic, who was born in 1917.

Joe eating spaghetti with his mother.

Fisherman's Wharf was an exciting place to grow up. Joe occasionally helped his father by cleaning and preparing the fishing nets. And like many other boys, he also held different odd jobs, such as selling newspapers, to earn spending money. Although these jobs did not pay well, he usually could earn the 25 cents he needed to go to the movies with his friends.

But most of Joe's time was spent playing sports. In fact, his first exposure to baseball came at the age of ten on the playgrounds of North Beach, playing with a softball on an asphalt surface. Joe was tall and thin, but strong for his age. From the start, he was an exceptionally good hitter—everyone wanted to be on Joe's team.

At this time, city and rural kids all over the United States played "sandlot" baseball, which was a game organized in a vacant lot or field. Joe and his friends played "horse-lot baseball." Not far from Fisherman's Wharf, there was a big empty lot where a local dairy company kept its horses and horse-drawn delivery wagons. Every day, the boys chased the horses away and made a field using rocks for bases. Since no one could afford a baseball glove, everyone played bare-handed. The kids used a taped ball, and an old oar acted as a bat.

Joe shows his bat to his dad, just before leaving for spring training in 1937.

6

Joe often played pick-up games on the weekends. Sometimes he would earn two dollars a game! By the time he was sixteen years old, he was known all over San Francisco as a talented baseball player.

Joe put a lot of energy into baseball, but he didn't put the same effort into his schoolwork. Like many children of immigrants, he had a difficult time understanding everything he was taught in school. At home, with his friends, around town, and on the wharf, Joe spoke Italian; in school, everyone spoke English. Learning was a frustrating experience for Joe. Since his family didn't have a lot of money, and since he didn't enjoy school, he decided to drop out when he was seventeen years old. He took a job in an orange juice factory, hoping to help out his family financially while he tried to decide what to do with his life.

Joe continued playing baseball, of course, but being an athlete seemed more like a hobby than a job. There were no major-league teams on the West Coast at the time, although there were many good minor-league teams. In fact, the major-league teams scouted these minor-league clubs heavily, and San Francisco was known as a hotbed of young talent.

Joe and Dom before the 1947 All-Star Game.

Ike Caveney, manager of the Seals, shows off his new player, seventeen-year-old Joe DiMaggio.

Joe got his big break in baseball in 1932, when he was still just seventeen years old. His older brother Vince, who was playing for the minor-league San Francisco Seals, convinced his manager that Joe could help the Seals in the infield. The Seals decided to give the younger DiMaggio a chance, and he played in three games that season. Joe hit well, and the Seals were impressed enough to ask him to report to spring training the following year.

The 1933 baseball season, Joe's minor-league rookie year, was a preview of the extraordinary career that was to follow. Joe had a .340 batting average for 187 games, with 28 home runs, 13 triples, and 45 doubles. He drove in 169 runs and scored 129 runs. Most amazing of all was Joe's 61-game hitting streak, a minor-league record that still stands today.

Soon, all sixteen major-league teams were sending scouts to watch Joe play. Because of the rules at that time, any major-league team interested in Joe DiMaggio would have to purchase him from the Seals in order to have him play for their team. By the end of the 1933 season, the Seals were asking for $75,000 for young Joe DiMaggio, a huge amount of money in those days.

Unfortunately, during the 1934 season Joe injured his knee and was on the disabled list for six weeks. This scared off many of the scouts. One scout, however, remained very interested in Joe—Bill Essick from the New York Yankees, who was a neighbor of the DiMaggios'. After much effort, Essick finally convinced the Yankees owners that DiMaggio was a great prospect. Better still for the Yankees, they could now get Joe for a much lower price.

The Yankees purchased DiMaggio for $25,000 and five players. As part of the deal, the Seals owner insisted that Joe play one more season for his minor-league team. The Yankees agreed but later regretted not having DiMaggio for the 1935 season. In that last season for the Seals, DiMaggio batted .398, with 34 home runs, 18 triples, and 48 doubles. He knocked in 154 runs and scored 173 runs. Meanwhile the Detroit Tigers won the American League pennant; the Yankees came in second.

The Yankees had signed other Italian-American ballplayers from San Francisco—Tony Lazzeri and Frank Crosetti were also from the area. These two ballplayers decided to try to help DiMaggio adjust to the major leagues and offered to drive him to spring training in Florida.

Because of DiMaggio's outstanding play in the Pacific Coast League, his major-league debut was eagerly awaited by the New York press and fans alike. Although Lazzeri and Crosetti looked out for their young friend, the quiet DiMaggio was a little overwhelmed by all the attention. The first spring training game went well for Joe, but during the second game he injured his foot sliding into second base. The injury sidelined him for a few weeks, forcing him to miss opening day. Although Joe would have preferred to play, he was relieved when some of the attention and hype cooled down.

Joe DiMaggio's first major-league game took place on May 3, 1936. He played left field and batted third in the lineup, ahead of the great Lou Gehrig. That first day in the major leagues, Joe hit a triple and two singles. The other players and fans took note: perhaps this kid really would live up to his advance billing.

Lou Gehrig and Joe DiMaggio during Joe's rookie season.

DiMaggio lived up to his reputation in the field as well. On May 8, several days after his debut, the Yankees were leading the Detroit Tigers 6–5 in the bottom of the ninth inning. With a man on third, Charlie Gehringer hit a fly ball to DiMaggio. Joe made the catch and threw out the runner at home with a brilliant throw.

Joe DiMaggio is remembered as one of the greatest center fielders of all time, but he actually began his Yankees career as a left fielder. The Yankees moved the fleet-footed rookie to center before the end of the 1936 season.

New York's "Murderers' Row," a lineup of powerful hitters, gets ready for the 1936 World Series.

Joe's first major-league home run came two days later, on May 10, against the Kansas City Athletics. On June 24, DiMaggio hit two home runs in one inning against the Chicago White Sox, tying a major-league record. With great hitting and impeccable fielding, DiMaggio was a shoe-in to play right field in the All-Star Game that year.

Following the All-Star Game, DiMaggio and his team continued to rough up the rest of the league. For the first time since 1932, the Yankees were in control of first place. By the end of the season, they had a record of 102 wins and 51 losses, placing them 19½ games ahead of the second-place Tigers. Lou Gehrig was the MVP of the league, hitting .354 with 49 home runs and 152 RBI. Tony Lazzeri hit .287 with 14 home runs and 109 RBI. George Selkirk hit .308 with 18 home runs and 107 RBI. Bill Dickey hit .362 with 22 home runs and 107 RBI. And the young rookie from San Francisco, Joe DiMaggio, hit .323 with 29 home runs and 125 RBI.

The Yankees continued their winning ways in the postseason, meeting the New York Giants in the World Series. It was the first time in thirteen years—since the days of Babe Ruth—that the two teams battled for the world championship.

The Giants won the first game 6–1, behind the exceptional pitching of Carl Hubbell. President Franklin D. Roosevelt was one of the 43,543 fans in attendance at game two who watched DiMaggio chase a long fly ball deep into center field for the final out in an 18–4 Yankees win. Much to the delight of their fans, the Yankees won the series, four games to two.

In addition to a superb performance in the field, Joe DiMaggio got 9 hits in 26 at bats for a .346 average. Bill Terry, manager of the Giants, commented on the rookie's contribution: "I've always heard that one player could make the difference between a losing team and a winner, and I never believed it. Now I know it's true." As it turned out, this was just the beginning of another Yankees dynasty; in his thirteen seasons with the Yankees, DiMaggio helped take them to the World Series ten times. They won nine of those series.

By the time the 1936 baseball season was over, Joe had been away from home for eight months. When he finally returned to San Francisco after the World Series, he was a hero. Joe rode through the streets in an open convertible with the mayor and was cheered by thousands. He also was able to move his family from their small apartment to a large stone house in the Marina district.

The rookie sensation.

Joe helped his family in other ways, too. He invested in a restaurant on Fisherman's Wharf called Joe DiMaggio's Grotto and put his brother Tom in charge of running it. He helped his brother Mike buy another fishing boat to expand the fleet. The rest of Joe's family helped him handle the attention he continued to receive—including the twenty or more fan letters that arrived each day—despite his desire to stay out of the limelight.

Joe's brother Tom also served as his business manager and helped him negotiate his contracts with the Yankees owners. In those days, players did not have agents or a players' union to represent their interests. There was no such thing as free agency; once a player signed with a team, the team could pay that player whatever salary it wanted to, or trade the player without his approval. The only leverage the players could apply was to withhold their services— meaning they would not play until they received the salaries they wanted.

The country was in the middle of the Great Depression. People who were lucky enough to have jobs often made about $14 a week. Joe DiMaggio received $8,500 in his rookie year and was holding out for $17,500 to start his second year. In fact, five of the World Champion New York Yankees were holding out for more money. Perhaps they deserved these salary increases, but some fans resented the ballplayers who asked for so much money in a time when so many were sacrificing. Joe eventually signed for approximately $15,000 that year, but he felt his reputation was unfairly tarnished because of the contract dispute.

DiMaggio decided to prove he was worth every penny and followed his outstanding rookie year with another incredible campaign. He led the majors in home runs with 46 and cemented his status as a star. Fans in every ballpark the Yankees visited came out to see him play and tried to get his autograph. For a shy young man, this attention was flattering but sometimes difficult to handle.

Joe soon discovered just how fickle fans could be, however. After the 1937 season, the Yankees offered DiMaggio a contract for $25,000, but Joe was asking for $40,000. The Yankees owners, who knew how to use the media to promote their interests, denounced DiMaggio publicly. He came across as a selfish, greedy player.

It was hard for Joe to defend himself. He stuck to his principles, sitting out all of spring training. Finally, after the third game of the regular season, he gave in. He sent a telegram to Colonel Ruppert, one of the Yankees owners, which read, "Your terms accepted. Leave at 2:40 P.M. Arrive Saturday morning."

Mel Ott and Joe Moore of the Giants, with Joe DiMaggio and Lou Gehrig of the Yankees, joke around before the first game of the 1937 World Series.

Ruppert gloated to the press, and when DiMaggio returned to play he was booed on the field. The Yankees had succeeded in their campaign to create fan resentment against DiMaggio. Joe was deeply hurt by the fans' response. "I hear the boos," he said, "and I read in the papers that the cheers offset them, but you can't prove that by me. All I ever hear is boos."

But once again, Joe won back the devotion of the fans with his outstanding play. On July 4, 1937, he hit a grand slam home run, and the crowd went wild. As *The New York Times* reported, "The stands shook with shouts and stomping, a deafening crescendo of shrieks, cheers, whistling, and hand-clapping."

DiMaggio opens his 1938 season with a single.

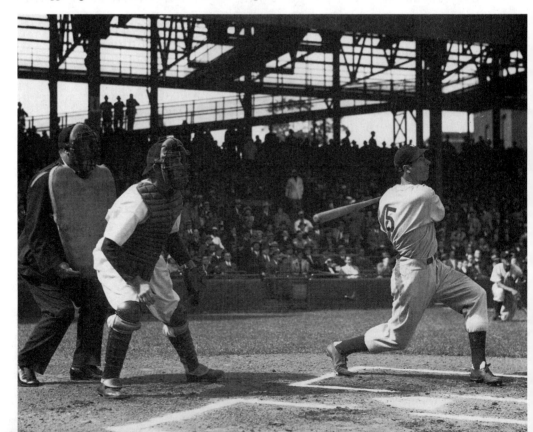

As a bachelor, Joe spent most of his free time in New York at Toots Shore's, a restaurant and club where sports stars and reporters hung out. He had a group of friends and admirers who traveled with him wherever he went. After he married movie actress Dorothy Arnold in 1934, Joe and his wife became friends with Yankees pitcher Lefty Gomez and his wife, June O'Dea, who was also an actress. The Yankees heroes and their wives made a stylish foursome around town.

Best of all, Joe and the Yankees continued to dominate baseball. During DiMaggio's first four seasons, the Yankees won four American League pennants by a combined 59 games, and four World Series by a combined record of 16–3. But in 1940 the Yankees got off to a slow start, as Joe was forced to sit out the beginning of the season with a knee injury. The Yankees chased Detroit and Cleveland all season but finished two games out of first place.

Bill Dickey (Yankees), Hank Greenberg (Tigers), and Joe DiMaggio (Yankees) before the 1939 All-Star Game.

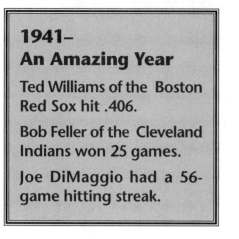

1941–
An Amazing Year

Ted Williams of the Boston Red Sox hit .406.

Bob Feller of the Cleveland Indians won 25 games.

Joe DiMaggio had a 56-game hitting streak.

Joe was determined to lead his team to victory again in 1941. But even he never imagined what would happen that magical season.

Nineteen forty-one would turn out to be one of the greatest years ever in baseball history. Three of the game's best players, Ted Williams, Bob Feller, and Joe DiMaggio, all would have remarkable seasons.

In retrospect, someone should have seen Joe's incredible hitting streak coming. After his 61-game hitting streak for the San Francisco Seals of the Pacific Coast League, DiMaggio proved he was no fluke. In 1936, his rookie year with the Yankees, he had a hitting streak of 18 games; in 1937, he had a 22-game streak; and in 1938, another of 23 games. Even before the start of the 1941 season, Joe hit safely in the last 19 games of spring training, and then the first 8 games of the regular season.

The New York Yankees game on May 15, 1941, was just like many others—Joe DiMaggio got a hit and knocked in a run. But after dominating baseball for five years, the Yankees had dropped to third place. The Yankees captain, Lou Gehrig, was dying of a terrible disease called amyotrophic lateral sclerosis, or ALS. Across the ocean, Germany was bombing Great Britain and invading Russia; Americans knew war was looming. For all these reasons, there were only 9,040 fans at Yankee Stadium that day to watch the beginning of a miracle.

Joe at bat in the 1941 All-Star Game.

It would be more than two months before Joe would have another hitless game. By the time the streak reached 20 games, sportswriters across the country were giving daily updates to their audiences. When DiMaggio broke George Sisler's modern-day record of 41 games, then Willie Keeler's all-time record of 44 games, radio stations interrupted their broadcasts to spread the news. For an anxious, concerned nation on the brink of war, Joe's streak was a more than welcome distraction. Even fans who despised the Yankees began cheering for Joe.

The very next day after the streak ended, DiMaggio singled and doubled off Bob Feller of the Cleveland Indians. This started a 16-game hitting streak—which means Joe hit safely in an incredible 72 out of 73 games!

On June 29, 1941, Joe slashes the single that broke George Sisler's record and extends his streak to 42 games.

During these weeks, the twenty-six-year-old DiMaggio solidified his reputation as a quiet, steely leader. Although the attention was difficult for the shy man, Joe remained cheerful and relaxed. Roommate Lefty Gomez had a much harder time, however: "Joe was calm, but every day after 44, I threw up my breakfast."

The excitement continued to build as Joe's streak reached 50 games and more. It ended on July 17 in Cleveland, before a cheering crowd of 67,468 fans. "I'm glad it's over," Joe said simply after the game.

During his streak, the Yankees had won 41 games and lost 13, with 2 ties. They climbed from fourth place, 5¹/₂ games back, to first place. The team continued on a tear the rest of the season, winning 101 games and finishing ahead of the second-place Red Sox by 17 games.

The Yankees beat the Brooklyn Dodgers in the World Series, four games to one. Joe finished the season as the major-league leader in runs batted in (125) and was named Most Valuable Player for the second time in his career. In the MVP voting, Joe finished just ahead of his rival Ted Williams, who hit .406 that season—another feat that has not been surpassed to this day.

Joe's off-season was also joyous: his son, Joseph Paul DiMaggio, Jr., was born on October 23, 1941. Six weeks later, however, the Japanese attacked Pearl Harbor, and the United States declared war on Germany and Japan.

Because so many players were eligible for the draft, professional baseball began to feel the effects of World War II as soon as the 1942 baseball season started. DiMaggio had another fine year for the Yankees as they finished first in the American League. For the only time in his career, however, the Yankees lost the World Series. Joe's personal life was also taking a turn for the worse; he and Dorothy Arnold decided to end their three-year marriage.

DiMaggio's 56-Game Hitting Streak by the Numbers

- Began on May 15, 1941; ended on July 17, 1941
- 223 at bats
- 91 hits: 56 singles, 16 doubles, 4 triples, and 15 home runs
- .408 batting average
- 21 walks; hit by a pitch twice
- Struck out only 7 times
- 56 runs scored
- 55 runs batted in

Joe and Dominic pose with Ted Williams (center) before Opening Day, 1942, in Yankee Stadium.

Sgt. Joe DiMaggio and Chief Specialist Pee Wee Reese (Dodgers) before a Central Pacific Area championship game during World War II.

On December 3, 1942, DiMaggio enlisted in the Army Air Force. He was suffering from the onset of severe ulcers and spent the war years in Honolulu, Hawaii, playing center field for the Seventh Army Air Force team. During the war, generals and admirals stationed all over the world staged baseball and football games using the professional athletes who were in the armed services. The games provided some brief moments of enjoyment for the soldiers away from their homes.

Joe was discharged from the Army on September 14, 1945, after the war ended. By November 20, he was back in New York to meet with the new owners of the Yankees. These owners welcomed Joe back with an open checkbook and no dispute over his contract.

Just released from the service, Joe visits the clubhouse with his son, Joe, Jr., and his first wife, Dorothy Arnold.

Like many players who were out of condition from being in the armed services, DiMaggio had a below-average season. He hit 20 home runs in the first 41 games, but only 5 for the rest of the season. Joe's batting average was just .290, and he missed 22 games with injuries.

At the beginning of the 1947 season, DiMaggio sat out a few games recovering from a bone-spur operation on his left heel. He played the season with another painful bone spur still in his right heel. Although his offensive statistics were still below his prewar years (.315 BA, 20 HR, 97 RBI), his fielding was sparkling—only one error in 141 games. Joe was elected Most Valuable Player for the third time, beating out Ted Williams in a hotly contested race. The Yankees met the Dodgers again in the World Series and won in a close seven-game series.

DiMaggio played most of the 1948 season with pain from the bone spur in his right heel. To his teammates, he was the quiet leader of the Yankees. In fact, Joe had become the conscience and personification of the Yankees. He lectured the younger players, such as Joe Page and Yogi Berra, and led them through his examples of hard work and good sportsmanship.

Joe kicks up a cloud of dust sliding into third against the Washington Senators in 1948.

During the 1948 season, Joe also led the American League with 39 home runs and 155 RBI. Despite his physical pain, DiMaggio played 153 games of the 154-game season. He also passed the 300 career-home-run mark, leading active players in career home runs.

The Yankees team did not fare so well, however. By the last series of the season, in Boston, the Yankees had been eliminated from the pennant race. Bucky Harris, the Yankees manager, knew how painful Joe's bone spurs were. He told Joe to sit out the series.

But Joe wouldn't hear of it. He did not want the fans to think he was favoring the Red Sox (who were in a pennant race with the Indians) because his brother Dom was on the team. Joe got three hits—including a home run—in the first game and went four for five in the next game. On his last hit he could only limp to first base. Joe left the game and received a standing ovation from the Boston fans—the very fans who loved to hate the Yankees.

During the off season, DiMaggio realized that his heel was not getting better. Mel Allen, the Yankees radio announcer, said, "For the first time he began to think he was through, finished, washed up as a ballplayer." Joe missed the first 65 games in 1949, but the Yankees' troubles ran even deeper. In the beginning of the season, Joe and Joe Jr. were featured on the cover of *Look* magazine. The article was titled "Is the Yankee Empire Crumbling?" The article concluded that the Yankees needed rebuilding and that "they will never again dominate baseball as they did for a quarter of a century."

In 1949, Johnny Mize joins DiMaggio and the Yankees from the Giants.

The Yankees certainly proved this prediction wrong—they went on to win ten American League pennants and seven World Series in the next twelve years! And it all started the very day in 1949 when Joe DiMaggio woke up and discovered the pain in his heel had disappeared.

On June 28, Joe started a game for the first time that season. He hit a single his first time up, and a home run the next time. Then DiMaggio hit two home runs the next day, and another on the following day as the Yankees swept a series from the Red Sox. Joe was back with a vengeance, and so were the Yankees.

October 1, 1949—Joe DiMaggio Day at Yankee Stadium. Joe poses with brother Dom, his mother, brother Tom, and Joe, Jr.

By the end of the summer, Joe's heel was causing him a great deal of pain once again. Nevertheless, Joe played well and kept the Yankees in the pennant race.

The season came down to the final two games against Boston in Yankee Stadium. The Red Sox had a one-game lead. A huge crowd of 69,551 crammed the stadium for "Joe DiMaggio Day." His brothers Dominic and Tom, his mother, and his son stood next to Joe as he was honored on the field before the first game of the series. Mrs. DiMaggio's loyalties must have been divided, for only one of her sons would be going on to the World Series.

The Yankees won the game to set the stage for a showdown in the last game of the season. In the top half of the ninth, with the Yankees leading 5–0, the Red Sox began a rally and scored three runs. After Bobby Doerr hit a triple over DiMaggio's head, an injured Joe called a time-out and took himself out of the game so he would not be a defensive liability. The crowd gave him a standing ovation as he hobbled to the bench, and the Yankees held on to win 5–3.

The Yankees beat the Dodgers once again in the Series, but Joe finished the season in a state of exhaustion. To the fans, though, he was a true hero, coming back after missing half the season with an injury and leading his team to greatness.

The 1950 season began with the Yankees grooming a new crop of stars—Mickey Mantle, Whitey Ford, and Billy Martin were all trying to win positions on the team. Casey Stengel, the manager, liked to platoon his players. Joe became a little annoyed when he was asked to play first base for one game, when he was switched to the number-five hitting position, and again when Stengel rested him for a few days in August.

When DiMaggio returned to the lineup after this unwanted break, he took his frustration out on the opposing pitchers. The thirty-five-year-old star hit .400 for the last two weeks of August, and .373 in September. Joe finished the season with a .301 average, 32 home runs, and 122 RBI. Once again he led the Yankees to the pennant, and they won another World Series, sweeping the Philadelphia Phillies in four games.

Joe gets ready to face the Phillies in the 1950 World Series.

Despite his great record in 1950, Joe opened the 1951 season hinting that this would be his final year. The press speculated how the Yankees and Stengel would face the dilemma. Would they play the rising young star Mickey Mantle in center field, or continue to play DiMaggio?

Stengel decided to play DiMaggio in center and Mantle in right, but neither got off to a great start. Mantle had problems with big-league pitchers and struck out frequently, finally being sent back down to the minors for six weeks. DiMaggio once again fought injuries and played in only 116 games. With final statistics of a .263 batting average, 12 home runs, and 71 RBI, the season was by far Joe's least successful.

But the Yankees were still loaded with talent, and they won the pennant by five games over the Indians. Then they went on to defeat the New York Giants in the World Series, four games to two.

After the season, the Yankees owners offered Joe a $100,000 contract—no strings attached. This meant that Joe would get paid even if he were unable to play. But Joe flatly refused. On December 11, 1951, the Yankees held a press conference to announce Joe DiMaggio's retirement. When asked for a reason why he was calling it quits, Joe simply said, "I just don't have it anymore."

★ ★ ★ Joe DiMaggio Career Statistics ★ ★ ★

1,736 games played
.325 career batting average
2,214 total hits
389 doubles
131 triples
361 home runs
1,390 runs scored
1,537 RBI
10 American League pennants in his 13-year career
9 World Series Championships

- 3 American League MVP awards: 1939, 1941, 1947
- 61-game hitting streak for the San Francisco Seals in 1933—still the minor-league record
- The only player in major-league history with more than 300 home runs (361) and less than 400 strikeouts (369) in his career
- Among the top five players in ten different offensive categories (hits, runs, doubles, triples, home runs, total bases, RBI, extra-base hits, batting average, and slugging percentage) on the Yankees' all-time list
- Elected to the Hall of Fame in 1955

Joe enjoyed retirement in San Francisco. He had met an actress named Marilyn Monroe, and the two became close friends. Gossip columns frequently featured items about the baseball star and the beautiful Monroe.

Joe and Marilyn Monroe attend a movie premiere.

Joe and Marilyn leaving City Hall after their wedding ceremony.

On January 14, 1954, Joe and Marilyn got married secretly in the chambers of the municipal court judge in San Francisco. Unfortunately for DiMaggio, someone had tipped off the press. A hundred or so reporters and photographers were waiting for them outside the judge's chambers, and hundreds more people swarmed Joe's car outside.

Life was hard for the couple. There was intense public interest in their every move, and their lifestyles were simply not compatible. A short nine months later they were divorced. However, the two remained close friends. After Marilyn's death in 1962, Joe took charge of her funeral. He also arranged to have fresh roses placed on her grave each week for years to come.

Joe remained in the public eye as a player as well. Despite his remarkable career and achievements, DiMaggio was not elected to the Hall of Fame the first time he was eligible—or even the second. Finally, in 1955, he was chosen for baseball's greatest honor.

DiMaggio had brief periods of involvement with baseball after he retired. He served as executive vice president and "special coach" of the Athletics in 1968 and 1969 after Charley Finley moved the team to Oakland. He also served on the board of directors of the Baltimore Orioles from 1980 to 1988.

For the most part, however, Joe kept to himself and his small circle of family and friends. In retirement he enjoyed the best of both his worlds—he was able to lead the private life he cherished, but he also had the opportunity to make appearances and be in the public eye when he chose. His reputation as a trustworthy, honorable man made DiMaggio a highly sought-after spokesperson for products and causes.

On October 12, 1998, Joe was admitted to the Memorial Regional Hospital in Hollywood, Florida. Two days later, he had surgery to remove cancer from his lung. After the operation he developed serious complications and spent periods of time in a coma. Fortunately, his condition improved, and he was released from the hospital in January.

The Yankees' owner, George Steinbrenner, visited Joe at home to remind him that he had a date to throw out the first pitch for the Yankees' season opener. Joe had a sheet of paper on the wall of his bedroom with "April 9" written on it. He was proud to be asked to throw out the first pitch.

But on March 8, 1999, Joe died at home. He was eighty-four years old. People all over the country mourned his death. The city of New York changed the name of one of its major roads, the West Side Highway, to the Joe DiMaggio Highway in his honor.

Joe and Andy Carey at the 1959 Yankees Old Timers' Day.

On Sunday, April 25, 1999, the Yankees held a ceremony to unveil Joe's monument in Monument Park, an area beyond left field in Yankee Stadium where Yankees heroes are immortalized. At the celebration, the songwriter Paul Simon sang his famous song "Mrs. Robinson," whose well-known lyrics include a mention of Joe DiMaggio.

Joe had once said that while he felt flattered to be mentioned in the song, he did not really understand what the words meant. Everyone in Yankee Stadium understood that day, however, as Paul Simon's voice drifted over the outfield:

Joltin' Joe has left and gone away...

For millions of baseball fans through the years, Joe DiMaggio represented the ideal hero. Calm and reserved, determined and graceful, talented and hard-working, Joe led his team and his country to greater heights through his extraordinary play. Truly a hero for all ages, Joe DiMaggio will live in the hearts of baseball fans forever.

Joe throws the first pitch at Opening Day 1998 in Yankee Stadium.

THE STREAK

On May 15, 1941, DiMaggio's first-inning single scored a run against the Chicago Cubs to start the streak.

On the next day, DiMaggio hit a tremendous home run into the left-center field bleachers in the third inning. In the ninth inning he hit a triple and later scored as the Yankees went on to win 6–5.

On May 17, the Yankees managed to get only five hits off Chicago's John Rigney, but DiMaggio had one of them, a second-inning single.

The following day, the Yankees defeated the St. Louis Browns 12–2. DiMaggio went three for three.

May 19 was the fifth game of the streak. DiMaggio hit a double in the seventh inning, and Bill Dickey hit a homer to bring his own hitting streak to 20 games.

Joe rounds first base after tying George Sisler's record 41-game hitting streak.

On May 20, Elden Auker of the Browns bested Joe with his submarine pitch—until the eighth inning, when Joe lined a single to center.

The next day the Detroit Tigers came to town, leading the Yankees in the standings. Joe singled in a run in the first inning and did the same in the ninth to tie the game. The Yankees won 5–4 in ten innings.

On May 22, DiMaggio came to the plate in the seventh inning without a hit. He singled off Archie McKain, rounded first, hustled back, and slid in the mud, just avoiding the tag.

On May 23, the Yankees played the Boston Red Sox. The game was tied 9–9 when the umpires called the game due to darkness. Although this game did not count in the standings, players' individual statistics did count. Joe had hit a single in the eighth inning.

In the seventh inning of the next game, Joe managed to hit a single to bring the streak to ten games.

In 1935, the Cincinnati Reds introduced night baseball at Crosley Field. In 1938, the first night game was played at Ebbets Field, the home of the Brooklyn Dodgers. Shibe Park in Philadelphia followed in 1939, and in 1940 Municipal Stadium in Cleveland, Comiskey Park in Chicago, Sportsman's Park in St. Louis, and the Polo Grounds in New York joined the night-game revolution.

On May 25, the Red Sox stole the show, with Ted Williams getting four hits and raising his average to .404 and pitcher Lefty Grove earning career win 296. But Joe ran the streak to 11 games with a single in the first.

May 26 was an off day, as the Yankees played their Norfolk, Virginia, minor-league team. It's a good thing this game didn't count—Joe popped up twice, walked once, and left the game after seven innings. Against the Washington Senators the next day, however, Joe got three singles and a home run as he went four for five and scored three runs.

The first night game played in Griffith Stadium, home of the Senators, occurred on May 28, 1941. The Yankees had a little trouble adjusting to the lights and were losing 3–1 in the eighth inning. Then DiMaggio hit a triple, and George Selkirk hit a pinch-hit grand slam as the Yankees scored five runs and won 6–5.

DiMaggio had another close call on May 29. He slammed a pitch straight into home plate. The ball bounced high and came down near third base—a Baltimore chop. Joe hustled down the first base line, barely beating the throw.

The Yankees and Red Sox split a doubleheader on May 30. DiMaggio walked twice in the first game, then lined a single to right field in the ninth inning. In the second game DiMaggio had a sore neck and shoulder, which resulted in four errors—easily the worst defensive performance of his career. But luck was with him at the plate, when right fielder Pete Fox lost his fly ball in the sun and it fell for a double in the fifth inning.

On June 1, the Yankees and Cleveland played a doubleheader. DiMaggio hit a single in the third inning of the first game. He went into the eighth inning of the second game before hitting a hard line drive that glanced off the third baseman's glove to keep the streak alive at 18 games.

On June 8, Ted Williams ended a 23-game hitting streak. Williams would admit later that he kept track of DiMaggio's streak. He once said, "I was always conscious of the other guy. Usually the guy was Joe DiMaggio."

The following day, the Indians' Bob Feller also had a streak going—30 scoreless innings in a row. The Yankees would spoil his streak in the second inning but went on to lose the game 7–5. DiMaggio got a single and a double off the fireballer.

After the game, the Yankees took the train to Detroit, where they found out that Lou Gehrig had died—seventeen days short of his thirty-eighth birthday.

Before the game on June 3, the teams lined up for a moment of silence in honor of Gehrig. Detroit won 4–2, but DiMaggio led off the fourth inning with a home run.

On June 5, Joe tripled into the left-field corner in the sixth inning to run the streak to 21 games.

In St. Louis on June 7, the Yankees scored five runs in the ninth to win 11–7. DiMaggio wound up with three singles.

In another doubleheader on June 8, DiMaggio hit two home runs in the first game and a double and a home run in the second game for a seven-RBI day.

Joe survived another close call on June 10 in Chicago by hitting a hard grounder to third in the seventh inning. Dario Lodigiani, an old family friend from San Francisco, knocked it down but could not make the throw.

DiMaggio extended his streak by hitting a single off Thornton Lee on June 12. Later, with the game 2–2 in the tenth, Joe smashed a home run to win the game.

The Yankees opened at home against Cleveland on June 14. All kinds of streaks were on the line: DiMaggio's 26-game hitting streak; the team streak of 9 consecutive games with at least one home run; a 5-game winning streak for the Yankees; Bob Feller's 8 straight wins; and a 6-game winning streak for the Indians. Most important, the Indians were fighting to stay in first place. A cheering crowd of 44,161 saw the Yankees win 4–1, and DiMaggio hit a double to right field to increase his streak to 27 games.

All the Yankees streaks continued in the game on June 15. Joe hit a homer into the upper deck in left field to extend his streak to 28 and the Yankees home-run streak to 11 games. They won 3–2.

Joe DiMaggio tied the Yankees record for a hitting streak at 29 on June 16 with a double in the fifth inning. The two men he tied were both on the field: Earl Combs was coaching first base for the Yanks, and Roger Peckinpaugh was the manager of the Indians. The Yankees homered for the twelfth game in a row and ran their winning streak to 8 games.

With the White Sox in town on June 17, the Yankees' winning streak came to an end, but Joe got another lucky break. In the seventh inning he hit a hard grounder to short, which took a bad hop at the last minute and skipped over Luke Appling's shoulder. Everyone in the ballpark immediately looked up to the official scorer, knowing this could be it. It was scored a hit; Joe had now hit safely in 30 straight games.

Joe and teammate Red Ruffing stretch before a game.

On June 18, Joe kept the streak going with a bloop single just out of Appling's reach. On June 19, Joe hit two singles and a home run.

With the Tigers in town on June 20, DiMaggio hit three singles and a double. He also made a tremendous catch off Rudy York's 450-foot drive to deep center field. The streak was now at 33 games. Joe would later comment that he never paid much attention to the streak until this point: "I didn't really warm up about this thing until the thirty-third game."

On June 21, for the third straight game, Joe got a hit his first time up with a looping single over first base.

DiMaggio drove a home run to right center to carry his streak to 35 games on June 22. The team home-run streak was now at 18 games, breaking the record set by the Tigers just one year earlier.

Although the Yankees won 9–1 on June 24, DiMaggio had a tough day. Finally, in the eighth inning, he drilled a single over the head of the shortstop. After the game a reporter asked if it would jinx him to talk about the close call. "Heck, no," Joe replied. "Voodoo isn't going to stop me. A pitcher will."

DiMaggio hit a single in the fourth inning the next day to keep the streak alive.

On June 26, submarine pitcher Eldon Auker faced the Yankees. DiMaggio flied out to left in the second inning, then grounded out in the fourth and again in the sixth. The Yankees were leading in the bottom of the eighth, and it looked like Joe might not get another chance to hit. Then with one out, Red Rolfe on first, and DiMaggio on deck, Tommy Henrich was at bat. Henrich realized a double play would end the streak. He asked for permission to bunt and laid one down, advancing Rolfe to second. Joe lined the first pitch past third base into the corner for a double.

Joe demonstrates his batting stance.

Number 39 came more easily the following day as Joe hit a single off his first pitch in the first inning. He also hit a home run later in the game.

DiMaggio doubled in the fourth inning on June 28 to pull within one game of the modern record of 41 set by George Sisler.

On June 29, the Yankees played a doubleheader before a packed stadium in Washington. The press box was filled with reporters hoping to write history. Dutch Leonard, an unpredictable knuckle-baller, was pitching for the Senators. In the sixth inning, Joe laced a fastball into left-center field for a double, tying the record.

At the start of the second game, Joe went into the dugout to find his lucky "streak bat," but it was missing from the rack. Tommy Henrich had been using a borrowed bat of Joe's for several weeks and gave it back to DiMaggio. But after three hitless at bats, Joe began to get a little nervous. Then, in the seventh inning, after a brushback pitch, Joe lined a single to left to set a new major-league record. The Yankees also extended their home-run streak to 25 games and pulled ahead of the Indians into first place.

An unidentified man called after the Philadelphia game on July 3 to say he knew where Joe's missing bat was. A friend of his had taken it as a souvenir. "He meant no harm," the caller said. "He loves you, Joe." Joe simply said, "I want it back." The bat was returned immediately.

The team returned to New York on July 1 for two games with Boston. With 50,000 fans in the stands, Joe hit a grounder to third that was not fielded cleanly by Jim Tabor. DiMaggio hustled to beat the throw. To the dismay of some, the official scorer called it a hit, but Joe settled the issue with a clean hit in his next at bat. The Yankees' home-run streak ended during this first game. Joe singled in the first inning of game two, and the Yankees won 9–2.

In a game against Philadelphia the following day, Stan Spence caught Joe's first-inning bid for a home run. However, in the fifth Joe smacked one over the fence in left, extending the streak to 45 games.

On July 5, DiMaggio hit another home run off Philadelphia.

Before a doubleheader on July 6, the Yankees unveiled a monument to Lou Gehrig in center field. During the first game, DiMaggio assaulted Philadelphia with three singles and a double. He added a triple and a single in game two.

July 2, 1941—Joe hits a home run, extending his streak to 45 games.

Later that week, Joe got a double in the All-Star Game in Detroit. Although that hit did not count as part of the record, the next day he hit a single in the first inning in St. Louis to run the streak to 49 games.

On July 11 in St. Louis, Joe hit three singles and a home run.

On July 12, Joe doubled off Eldon Auker, the submarine pitcher.

In a doubleheader against Chicago on July 13, Joe got three singles off Ted Lyons in the first game and one single off Thornton Lee in the second game.

The next day, Joe broke his lucky bat when he hit a pop fly. Later in the game, using a replacement bat, he hit a single.

Joe singled and doubled off Edgar Smith on July 15, and the Yankees headed to Cleveland with the streak at 55 games.

The Yanks opened a series with the Indians on July 16. Joe singled off Al Milnar in the first and third innings, then doubled off Joe Krakauskas in the fourth. The streak was at 56 games.

America's obsession with the streak was reaching fever pitch. The largest crowd ever to see a night game in the major leagues (67,468) crowded Municipal Stadium in Cleveland on Thursday, July 17. Joe's roommate, Lefty Gomez, was pitching against Al Smith. In the first inning, Joe pulled a ball down the third-base line. It was fielded by Ken Keltner, who fired to first just in time to get Joe out. In his next at bat, Smith walked DiMaggio. The crowd was furious with the pitcher and booed long and loudly. In the seventh, DiMaggio pulled the ball to Keltner again, who repeated his fine play of the first inning and threw Joe out by a step. In the eighth inning, with the bases loaded and one out, DiMaggio came to bat again. Jim Bagby threw a fastball that DiMaggio hit hard to deep short. Lou Boudreau made a great catch and threw it to Ray Mack at second for one out. Mack wheeled and threw to Oscar Grimes at first to complete the double play. The Streak was over after 56 games. Joltin' Joe had made baseball history.